Original title:
Where Green Grows

Copyright © 2025 Creative Arts Management OÜ
All rights reserved.

Author: Rosalie Bradford
ISBN HARDBACK: 978-1-80581-894-6
ISBN PAPERBACK: 978-1-80581-421-4
ISBN EBOOK: 978-1-80581-894-6

Vibrant Echoes

In the meadow, the sheep do prance,
With wool so fluffy, they start a dance.
A cow in shades of polka dot,
Sips from a flower-filled teapot.

A rabbit wearing a dapper hat,
Challenges a snail in a race; how fat!
The sun is shining, everyone's a player,
Even the worms cheer, "Let's get louder!"

Where Life Blossoms

In the park, the squirrels play chess,
Arguing who's the best, I must confess.
A turtle shouts, "I'll make my move!"
But naps come first, that's how they groove.

The flowers giggle with colors bright,
Tickling the bees in their buzzing flight.
And ants parade, they think they're grand,
With tiny trumpets, the whole band!

A Green Reverie

A lizard lounges on a rock, so cool,
Practicing lines for the next big duel.
A ladybug in specs takes notes,
"Today, I'll rule—ay!" she proudly gloats.

The breeze tells jokes, in swaying trees,
While flowers bloom just to aim for bees.
A playful breeze, with its funny spin,
Whispers, "Hey, grass, let's throw a din!"

Flourishing Horizons

In the garden, a gnome just fell,
He yells, "Help me out, this is no hotel!"
As daisies giggle at the sight,
The grass joins in, what a funny flight!

A fox with shades struts on by,
With a wink and a smirk, oh my, oh my!
The frogs croak choruses, quite the show,
While crickets clap, they steal the glow!

Beneath the Canopy of Hope

Underneath the trees that sway,
A squirrel's dance makes my day.
He leaps, he hops, he takes a chance,
While I just sit and watch his dance.

The branches tickle my big head,
As I dodge a nut, it's lightly said.
If I had a tail like he,
I'd flip it proud for all to see!

Lullabies of the Leafy Realm

Crickets chirp a sweet old tune,
While frogs croak in a funky swoon.
A leaf dropped down, my hat it stole,
I guess it thought it had a role!

In giggles, bees buzz all around,
Mistaking my head for a flower crown.
When I swat, they make a scene,
I'm just a human, not a queen!

A Walk Through Flourishing Fields

Tripping over my own two feet,
Trying to dodge a playful beet.
He takes a turn, I lose my stride,
That little bug's got a lot of pride!

The daisies wink, the daisies cheer,
"Come and play, you've got no fear!"
But the grass is tall, it tickles my nose,
Sneezing loud like a garden hose!

Serene Whispers of Nature

Butterflies flirt in the sunny air,
While I trip over, unaware.
One lands on my nose, oh what a jest,
I think it wants me to take a rest!

The wind laughs softly through the trees,
Making the branches wave with ease.
And I chuckle too, for what a sight,
In this leafy realm, I feel just right!

The Whispering Leaves

The leaves were gossiping, quite the chat,
About the squirrel wearing a tiny hat.
They laughed at the flowers, such a silly bunch,
Who think they're the stars of a lunch-hour crunch.

A crow cawed loudly, drawing attention,
To the ridiculous tales of their own invention.
But when the wind blew, they'd quickly hush,
As the breeze carried secrets with a playful rush.

A Symphony of Sprouts

The little sprouts formed a quirky band,
Playing tunes to the rhythm of the land.
The carrots danced in a colorful jive,
While radishes tried to take a dive.

With peas as the chorus, singing out loud,
And corn as the drummer, oh so proud.
The vegetables swayed to the gardener's beat,
While weeds crept in, with two left feet.

In the Heart of Verdancy

In a patch so plush, a rabbit took a seat,
Sipping on tea, quite the dainty treat.
His friend the snail, moved slower by the day,
Said, 'You'll never win a race, or so they say!'

But the rabbit just chuckled, 'I'm here for the fun,
While you munch on leaves in the warm, bright sun!'
A gathering of critters, what a sight to see,
All weaving their tales by the old cherry tree.

Beneath the Emerald Canopy

Underneath the branches, a party took place,
With frogs in tuxedos, and turtles in lace.
The insects brought snacks, a fantastic spread,
Crickets drummed softly, filling hearts with dread.

They leapt and they twirled, a chaotic delight,
While fireflies glimmered, lighting up the night.
And if you listened closely, you'd hear the cheer,
'What a great night, until the dawn draws near!'

The Stillness of Blossom

Petals swirl like dancers,
In a breeze so light,
Bees in tiny trousers,
Buzzing with delight.

Squirrels play hide and seek,
A game that's never done,
Chasing tails, so to speak,
Under the warming sun.

Flowers wear their bright hats,
Strutting down the lane,
Talking gossip with the rats,
While they sip on rain.

In stillness there's such cheer,
But oh, the playful mess,
Nature's very own sphere,
Of whimsical excess.

Enchanted by Nature

A snail with dreams so big,
Plans to race the wind,
But trips on a twig,
His journey's just pretend.

Frogs in suits debate,
How to catch a fly,
While grasshoppers relate,
In leaps, not knowing why.

The leaves are giggling low,
In whispers soft and sly,
Tickled by the glow,
Of a dancing butterfly.

A picnic's all a joke,
With ants that steal the bread,
While nature plays the yolk,
On the snack we thought we spread.

Ferns and Fables

Ferns weave tales of old,
In shades of emerald green,
A story never told,
By squirrels quite unseen.

The crows hold court so grand,
With crowns made of twigs,
They plot their vast command,
And dance like silly pigs.

The toad sits quite astute,
On a log, full of quips,
With laughter absolute,
And wise old mossy tips.

In this leafy realm of play,
Mysteries float like dreams,
As nature finds a way,
To giggle at the seams.

Life's Lush Tapestry

Moss blankets the ground,
In a hug that holds tight,
While the plants spin around,
In a merry, leafy flight.

A raccoon dons a cap,
Thinking he's quite legit,
Stealing snacks with a slap,
In a clever little skit.

The daisies gossip low,
About the bugs so bold,
Who wear their stripes like show,
In a world of pure gold.

Threads of laughter entwine,
In this botanical tale,
Where the sun does align,
To tickle us without fail.

Murmurs of the Meadow

In a field where the daisies dance,
Bugs parade and squirrels prance.
A cow in boots, so full of cheer,
Sings off-key for all to hear.

The frogs wear hats, they croak in style,
A fashion show, they do compile.
Twirling grasshoppers leap and spin,
While ants boast of their meal within.

The wind whispers jokes to the trees,
Tickling leaves with playful breeze.
Butterflies flutter in comic delight,
Chasing shadows, oh what a sight!

So come and join this jolly spree,
In the wild, everyone's zany and free.
The meadow laughs under the sun,
A funny place where life's just fun.

Fragrant Secrets

Beneath the blooms, a secret stash,
Honeybees gossip and make a splash.
A daisies' joke makes the tulips snort,
While rosemary plots in a fragrant retort.

Here's a cat chasing after the scents,
Claiming mint leaves are worth the rents.
Lavender chuckles, tickles the air,
While thyme whispers, 'Do you even care?'

The garden gnomes giggle with glee,
Caught in a game of hide and seek, you see.
But when the dogs chase in their chase,
Garden chaos, oh what a race!

Among these plants, laughter will soar,
In every leaf, there's a tale in store.
With petals that blush, and herbs that cheer,
The secrets of fragrance, oh so dear.

As Nature Awakens

Morning breaks with a yawning tree,
Stretching branches like it's time for tea.
A snail scoots off with a snailish grin,
Saying, 'I'll get there, just let me begin!'

The dew drops giggle in sparkling light,
Painting the grass with diamonds bright.
A bird in pajamas sings off key,
While a hedgehog rolls, feeling so free.

Critters jive as the sun peeks through,
Dance like no one, just me and you.
A cucumber grins, it's ready for lunch,
'Pickle me crazy!' it says with a crunch.

As nature wakes, with fun in the air,
Life's little quirks are beyond compare.
A stage for humor, a play to unfold,
In this lively world, stories are told.

The Rhythm of the Roots

Underfoot, earth wears its shoes,
With roots that wiggle in funny hues.
A worm writes songs in the darkened soil,
Tapping to rhythms, no need to toil.

The beetles march, a marching band,
Playing their music across the land.
A dance-off starts beneath the ground,
As laughter erupts, a joy profound.

Mushrooms giggle, wearing tiny caps,
Hosting tea parties with little mishaps.
The groundhog laughs, eyeing the scene,
Says, 'Who knew soil could be so keen!'

In the hidden world beneath our gaze,
Is a carnival of earthy plays.
Roots sway and twist, with rhythm and cheer,
Life in the soil, oh so sincere!

Revelations in the Foliage

In a jungle of leaves, I trip and fall,
The squirrels laugh loudly, they see it all.
A raccoon points and gives me a wink,
I ponder my life while sipping some drink.

Birds are gossiping, perched on a limb,
Discussing my shoes, calling them dim.
One said they're trendy, a fierce new fad,
The other just snorted, said they look bad.

Ferns wave their fronds, so sassy and spry,
"Did you even try?" they tease with a sigh.
I nod and I smile, then slip on some moss,
Foliage fashion, now that's my boss!

Fluffy clouds giggle, shadows take flight,
Sunbeams dance joyfully, quite the sight.
Nature's a jester, playing her tricks,
In the leafy laughter, I find my kicks.

The Calm After the Rain

Puddles are mirrors, reflecting the sky,
A frog leaps on by, croaking out, "Hi!"
His princely demeanor, quite over the top,
But hey, in this world, we all might just flop.

The flowers are splashing, their colors ablaze,
A rebellious petal in a mischievous craze.
A snail moves on up, so slow and so sleek,
"I'll race ya!" I shout, "Though I feel quite weak."

Raindrops still dappling the grass with delight,
A bee's got a buzz that can start quite a fight.
He dances around, saying, "What's your game?"
I answer, "Just chillin', but I can't feel my fame."

But amidst all the laughter, the joyous refrain,
I spot a small worm who's found his domain.
He chuckles so loud, says, "Life's a cool ride!"
And with that, I join him, in puddles we glide.

Embraces of Nature's Carpet

Lush carpet of leaves, soft under my feet,
I step on a twig, now that's quite a feat.
The squirrels all cheer, a cacophony of glee,
I bow like a dancer, what a sight to see!

A toad croaks loudly from deep in the grass,
"Do watch your step, or you'll land on your… class!"
I chuckle and look, and behold, what a scene,
A picnic of ants, hosting quite the cuisine!

Moss hugs the stones, just a tad bit too tight,
It whispers, "You're welcome, but not for the night."
Raccoons come waltzing, a band of mischief,
I join their parade, a quirky relief.

Nature's embrace brings a whimsical cheer,
In this wondrous world, I've nothing to fear.
I tumble and roll, laughter fills up my soul,
The carpet of green is my heart's very goal.

Tales from the Lively Thicket

In thicket so lively, the critters convene,
They plot and they plan like a great movie scene.
A owl gives a wink, all wise and aloof,
As the rabbit hops past, nearly flies off the roof.

The hedgehogs are gossiping, sharing some lore,
While the bees trade their secrets, oh what a score!
A deer prances by with a theatrical flair,
"Who needs a stage? I've got this fresh air!"

The bushes are buzzing, with antics galore,
A chameleon just squawked, "Look, there's a door!"
I peer through the leaves, and there I do see,
An otter in shades, sipping chilled rosé.

The thicket is vibrant, a riot of giggles,
With secrets and stories, and occasional wiggles.
Together we bask in this wild, playful land,
Where laughter and nature walk hand in hand.

Shades of Renewal

In a garden full of weeds,
Socks on the wrong feet,
I found a lettuce dancing,
To taste the sun's warm greet.

With a hat of bug repellent,
And shoes that squeak like ducks,
The flowers gossip gaily,
As I trip on hidden rucks.

A worm gave me advice,
To water wrong, not right,
And now I brew a salad,
That wiggles with delight.

In this patch of crazy greens,
I laugh and holler loud,
With every sprout's funny face,
I'm thoroughly proud!

Harmony in the Growing

The daisies sing in chorus,
While the broccoli does prance,
The carrots tell a story,
Of a radish's lost romance.

A sunflower wears glasses,
To see all the tiny bugs,
While a bean pole does the twist,
And gives the squashes hugs.

In my backyard bedlam,
The squirrels plot a raid,
They think they're super stealthy,
But my cat has them waylaid.

Laughter sprouts with each new leaf,
In this funny leafy show,
Nature's chatty plants unite,
In an uproariously green tableau!

Nature's Lush Palette

The potted plants wear colors,
Like a jester in disguise,
With pinks that clash with yellows,
And greens that improvise.

A cactus tried to paint me,
With spikes that went too far,
But I just used some humor,
And called it modern art!

The tulips giggle softly,
As bees buzz by to flirt,
While the mushrooms pull a prank,
And hide beneath my shirt.

In this canvas of mischief,
I find my heart is light,
As nature's funny palette,
Makes every day so bright!

Flowers of Resilience

The daisies stand like soldiers,
In veg beds full of pride,
They wear a crown of dirt clods,
And smile with joys inside.

A tulip told a joke that,
Made snails laugh through the rain,
While butterflies just fluttered,
Pretending not to strain.

Weeds wear the crown of glory,
And mock my every task,
Yet they have charm in folly,
And more than I could ask.

In this wild, bright patch of life,
I dance between the rows,
For laughter is the garden,
And that's how joy just grows!

Secrets of the Lush Meadow

In a meadow full of surprises,
Bunnies wear funny disguises.
With carrots tied like bowties,
They dance beneath the blue skies.

Squirrels juggle acorns with flair,
While flowers giggle without a care.
The bees hum tunes in their hive,
Buzzing about, oh so alive!

Dandelions puff with delight,
As gophers sneak, hoping they're right.
Each step a stomp, a boisterous cheer,
The gossip here is truly sincere.

Chipmunks hold a debate on a leaf,
With arguments simple, but beyond belief.
They giggle and wiggle in the warm sun,
This laughter, my friend, is just too fun!

Dance of the Sunlit Ferns

Ferns wiggle when the sun's ablaze,
They throw a party in so many ways.
With shadows that twist and twirl,
They invite all to join their whirl.

A ladybug leads in rhythm divine,
While grasshoppers hop, forming a line.
The beetles bring snacks, oh what a treat,
This dance floor is quite the feat!

The breeze sings softly through the leaves,
As the tiny creatures strap on their sleeves.
With a wink and a nod, they leap and glide,
In hilarity, they frolic with pride.

At twilight, the sun takes a bow,
But the ferns keep dancing, oh look at them now!
A midnight rave with fireflies in tow,
In this leafy party, the fun's never low!

The Cradle of Blossoms

In a cradle made of petals bright,
Every flower dreams of a colorful night.
Tulips wear hats, daisies wear shoes,
They play tag with the morning dews.

The roses recite poems, oh so grand,
While violets giggle, forming a band.
They strum on stems like guitars in bloom,
Creating a melody wrapped in perfume.

Butterflies waltz in polka-dot flair,
While sunflowers spin without a care.
Even the weeds get into the fun,
With choreography that's second to none!

With laughter echoing through the air,
This cradle of blossoms has love to share.
So come join the frolic, it's quite the scene,
A garden so merry, it's more than a dream!

Life Among the Ferns

In a world of green, the ferns reside,
With secrets and shadows they love to hide.
Snails wear their shells like hats on a spree,
As they take their time to drink herbal tea.

The frogs in their suits have begun to debate,
On who can jump highest, oh what a fate!
And crickets, they chirp in a rhythm so fine,
Announcing the start of their grand, nightly line.

Mice plot a picnic, but cheese is a must,
While ladybugs look at them, with a gust.
"Bring snacks," they chime, "for a feast most sweet,"
In this ferny realm, it's a laugh and a treat!

As day turns to night and the stars prance above,
Each leaf whispers secrets, all wrapped up in love.
In the life among ferns, joy finds its place,
With every green corner, there's laughter and grace!

Nature's Whispering Gallery

Amidst the trees so tall and free,
Squirrels chat quite busily.
A rabbit hops, a dance so slick,
Under the sun, a quick backflip!

Birds a-chatter with glee and cheer,
While a worm escapes their sneaky leer.
Leaves gossiping rustle all around,
Nature's secrets in whispers found.

A frog croaks jokes, quite ribbiting,
As butterflies join in, flitting and flitting.
Each flower laughs in colors bright,
In this gallery of pure delight!

So here we stand, quite bemused,
By all this fun, we're thoroughly amused.
Nature's stage, a comedy rare,
With critters performing everywhere!

Environments of Enchantment

In a meadow, bright and fair,
The insects waltz in sunshine's glare.
A butterfly slips, then loses its hat,
While a ladybug laughs, "Fancy that!"

Trees wear bows of mossy lace,
While bees zoom in a hurried race.
"Buzz off!" shouts a flower with flair,
In this drama played out without a care.

The grass tickles toes strolling by,
And a curious snail peeks, oh my!
A parade of critters, oh what a sight,
In this realm of joy, pure delight!

Where laughter blooms in every nook,
Environmental jokes in every book.
Tune in to nature, it's comedy grand,
In this whimsical, wild band!

Tides of Renewal

A stream giggles as it flows past,
With rocks as friends, it rolls so fast.
A fish jumps up, a splashy joke,
While in the reeds, a frog bespoke!

The sun dips low, casting a grin,
As crickets chirp in a lively din.
The breeze tells tales from way back when,
Of trees that danced with all their kin.

A snail writes poetry in the mud,
While ants throw a party, oh what a thud!
In the cycle of life, laughter abounds,
In these tides of joy, happiness found.

Each wave a chuckle, each ripple a tease,
Nature's humor flows through the trees.
So let's celebrate, dance with glee,
For in this world, wild and free!

The Pulse of the Wilderness

In the wild, things jump and run,
Every creature lives for fun.
A raccoon dons a mask with pride,
While squirrels play, their energy wide!

A wise old owl watching the show,
Chuckles softly, "Now, that's a glow!"
The deer prances in moonlit gleam,
Tripping over a twig, "Was that a dream?"

In this pulse, the rhythm is light,
As critters dance through day and night.
Nature's tempo never stops,
With a twist and turn, it flops and hops!

So listen close to the laughter all around,
In the wilderness, joy is found.
In every rustle, a quirk, a tease,
In this animated world, do as you please!

Overgrowth's Embrace

In a garden so wild and lush,
The weeds host a glorious crush.
Potatoes dance, tomatoes sing,
While squirrels plot their next big fling.

A rogue carrot shoots for the sky,
Waving at clouds that wander by.
The radishes gossip, oh my dear!
Telling tales that plant lovers fear.

Bumblebees buzzing with glee,
Making honey from the trees.
Under leaves where shadows play,
Snails audition for Broadway today!

So if you stumble upon this scene,
Know that chaos reigns where it's green.
A tangle of joy, a splash of mirth,
The happiest garden on this earth!

The Wonder of Wildness

In the thicket, a gopher's show,
Digging deep, much to its woe.
Poking its head, it slips in mud,
Then softens the ground, like a big, brown bud.

Grass blades whisper their cheeky tales,
Of squirrels stealing the long-tailed snails.
A bunny bounds, with a wiggly nose,
Dancing around in oversized clothes.

Dandelions laugh, petals aglow,
While stubborn kids tussle below.
With crickets' chirps and frogs' own croaks,
The wildness here is a joke that pokes!

So let your heart leap with this charm,
In a meadow, it's never a harm.
Life's a giggle in nature's embrace,
Join the party, and join the race!

Abundance Awaits

In the patch that's bursting with glee,
Pumpkins plotting a giant spree.
Every leaf's a canvas, quite broad,
Width of the harvest, oh my God!

The beetles host a family feast,
While ants strut like they're the least.
Fleas pull pranks on all the plants,
As fireflies dance in tiny pants.

Sprouts peek out with expectant bows,
Wondering what life owes, who knows?
Rabbits munch on salads galore,
Wishing for more, always more!

So grab your basket, join this fun,
Nature's buffet has just begun.
In rows of laughter, let's partake,
For a good chuckle's the best mistake!

Hearts of the Meadow

Meadow larks sing in clumsy flight,
Fumbling their words, a comical sight.
A patch of daisies, swaying in tune,
Playing host to a silly raccoon.

Butterflies flutter, munching on pie,
At a picnic of nectar, oh me, oh my!
The sun paints the world in laughter so bright,
While trolls under bridges engage in a fight.

The bubbling brook chuckles along,
Making ripples to hum a sweet song.
Worms throw a rave, digging down low,
In a slimy disco, putting on a show!

So wander these groves with a carefree heart,
Join in the jest, play your sweet part.
With every petal, every sprout,
The joy of the meadow is what it's about!

The Heart of Nature

Silly squirrels dance on trees,
Chasing tails in the warm breeze.
Flowers giggle in sunny rays,
While bees buzz by in a cheerful daze.

The brook spills secrets, oh so sweet,
With slippery fish doing flips on repeat.
Frogs recite jokes to the flies,
While turtles slowly plot their next surprise.

The sun paints the dew with a wink,
As birds debate on the best way to drink.
Nature's antics, a playful sight,
With laughter echoing day and night.

Echoes of the Forest

In the woods, trees wear grins,
Swinging branches, where fun begins.
Chipmunks chatter with cheeky flair,
As mushrooms giggle beneath their hair.

A fox tells tales of midnight quests,
While owls hoot jokes that never rest.
Leaves rustle softly with each pun,
Echoing laughter beneath the sun.

The breeze carries chuckles far and wide,
As nature's laughter takes a joy ride.
In shadows where sunshine can't chase,
Lies the forest's silly embrace.

In the Shade of the Oak

Beneath the oak, where wise folks sit,
Rabbits play games, never quit.
The acorns drop with a comic flair,
As squirrels plot, without a care.

Grass tickles toes as we play tag,
While butterflies zip like a colorful rag.
Sunbeams peek through the leafy crown,
As shadows dance in a funny gown.

With every breeze, a joke is spun,
Caterpillars laugh, oh what fun!
In the shade, life takes a break,
As chortles bounce with every shake.

The Color of Renewal

Painted petals in lively hues,
Dancing dreams to the morning blues.
Jokes of pollen, they share with glee,
As butterflies swirl, graceful and free.

In spring's embrace, the world's a jester,
Flowers wear hats, the brightest bester.
Bees tease blooms with a humming sound,
In the carnival of colors, joy abounds.

The rain drums laughter on thirsty ground,
While raindrops leap, a joyous round.
In every shade, life takes a cheer,
As smiles bloom in the atmosphere.

Glistening Grottoes

In a cave where mushrooms dance,
Far from the world, they prance.
With whispers and giggles so sly,
They laugh at the sun as it waves goodbye.

Bats wearing hats fly in disgrace,
Gargling echoes fill the space.
A mushroom thinks it's a sage,
Claiming wisdom found on every page.

Rats in tuxedos take the stage,
Reciting poetry, oh, so sage.
They twirl 'round in a jaunty spree,
In this grotto, you'll find glee.

Giggling ferns sway with flair,
While crickets argue who has the best hair.
It's a wild party of weird delight,
In a grotto, glowing bright at night.

Portraits of Abundance

In a field of veggies, what a sight,
Carrots wearing shades, oh, what a light!
Tomatoes blush with laughter so round,
While cabbage debates the best disco sound.

Zucchini struggles to find its groove,
Boogie-woogie moves are hard to prove.
Peas in a pod chuckle with cheer,
As radishes whisper, 'Don't look over here!'

Lettuce models, strutting their stems,
Claiming they're truly the botanical gems.
Eggplants giggle, swaying in grace,
While corn tries to win the best-dressed case.

Potatoes roll while onions cry,
'Why do they get all the attention?' they sigh.
In this cornucopia of silly art,
Nature's gallery makes the heart smart.

The Language of Leaves

Leaves gossip softly, fluttering in tune,
'Look at that flower, it thinks it's a boon!'
While whispering winds weave tales with flair,
Of bees stealing honey without a care.

The oak declares, 'I'm the tallest sage!'
But the willow retorts, 'You're stuck in your age!'
Bamboo chimes in, 'I'm bending with style!'
'You'd be cool too, if you'd loosen your pile!'

Maples blush in their vibrant red,
While pine with its needles curls up in bed.
They nod to the ground and wink with delight,
As earthworms throw parties under the night.

Together they gossip, a leafy brigade,
Telling wild stories, they've got it made.
In the breeze, they chuckle and sway,
Sharing secrets only leaves convey.

Serenade to the Wildflowers

In a meadow of colors, a band starts to play,
Wildflowers sway, putting on a display.
Daisies hum tunes that make butterflies swoon,
While poppies shake maracas and sing out of tune!

Sunflowers turn with hats made of sun,
Competing for rays, oh, the floral fun!
They giggle as fickle winds dance around,
Shivering petals, the wildest sound.

Bluebells ring in harmony's cheer,
While clovers play tag without any fear.
A dandelion whispers, 'Make a wish quick!'
As bees buzz along with a comic flick.

Petals twirl wildly in a pastel dance,
Sharing the joy of floral romance.
Oh, the wildflowers, a colorful choir,
Singing of laughter that never grows tired.

Roots in Rich Earth

In the soil, worms wiggle with glee,
They dance and twirl, quite carefree.
A rabbit sneezes, oh what a sight,
While carrots giggle, oh what a fright!

The beetroot blushes, all dressed in red,
While spinach whispers, "Can I play instead?"
A sunflower winks, in the summer breeze,
As daisies yell, 'Hey, look at me, please!'

The radish rolls, thinking it's cool,
While the chives form a leafy school.
A party erupts from roots to leaf,
Nature's humor, beyond belief!

With laughter amidst the patchy ground,
In this mad garden, joy is found.
Roots buried deep in the belly of fun,
Laughing together, they bask in the sun!

The Evergreen Embrace

Pine trees giggle in the summer heat,
While squirrels race, think it's a treat.
A bear takes a nap, snores with delight,
As the bushes chuckle at his sleepy sight.

The ferns fan their fronds like a fan,
Moss tickles the feet of anyone it can.
An owl hoots jokes from its high-up nest,
While the leaves rustle, 'We're the best!'

The evergreens boast, 'We're here for the long run,'
While young saplings giggle, 'We're just having fun!'
Tree trunks twist, engaging in jest,
In this jolly forest, laughter's the quest.

In a vibrant green hug, all join the show,
Nature's own circus, how wild and low!
In every shadow, a joke to embrace,
Under a canopy, joy finds its place!

Colors of the Hidden Grove

In a secret nook, mushrooms play peek,
Bright polka dots on their caps so chic.
Bumblebees buzz with a giggly hum,
While butterflies flutter, never feeling glum.

The ivy giggles, dressed in pastel,
With a friendly vine, it's an ivy carousel.
A chameleon jokes, popping colors bold,
While petals chuckle, 'We're not getting old!'

The creek bubbles up, sharing stories of cheer,
While frogs croak puns for all to hear.
Each hue in the grove blends wisdom and fun,
In the heart of the wild, laughter's never done.

Every shade sings in a playful dance,
As nature's palette spins in a chance.
In the hidden grove, where smiles do reign,
All the colors blend, no room for disdain!

A Tapestry of Tranquil Fields

In the open expanse, daisies pop up,
While a snail crawls, sipping dew from a cup.
Horses trot by, with manes that flow,
As the wind whispers secrets only they know.

The clouds float above, like fluffy balloons,
As grasshoppers tap out their funny tunes.
A butterfly sneezes, and petals burst wide,
Laughing at the joy that can't be denied.

The sunbeams wink through the leafy strands,
Tickling the flowers, forming goofy bands.
Every stalk sways to the light-hearted beat,
In this vibrant field, happiness is sweet.

The tapestry glimmers, a patchwork of glee,
Where every critter joins in harmony.
In tranquil waves, life takes its turns,
As nature giggles, and the heart just yearns!

The Lure of Mossy Glades

In shady spots, the ants march proud,
With tiny hats, they form a crowd.
A worm in dance, a twisty show,
While frogs croak loud, in a row they go.

The mushrooms gossip, hats on their heads,
Whispering secrets to fenced-up beds.
A squirrel in socks, so snazzy and bright,
Scampers past, what a silly sight!

Sudden rain makes all things slip,
A snail in boots takes a wild trip.
Who knew a puddle could cause such cheer?
At the banquet of bugs, it's feast time here!

Oh, mossy glades, with magic delight,
Where laughter dangles, both day and night.
Now join the fun, leave worries behind,
In the wild, there's joy of all kinds!

Breath of the Forest Floor

Underfoot lies a carpet of joy,
Mice in top hats, a tiny ploy.
With acorn snacks, they throw a bash,
And dance like mad in a whimsical flash.

The ferns wave flags in a leafy cheer,
While spiders spin tales that you can't hear.
A raccoon in rollerblades zooms on past,
Chasing a beetle, oh what a blast!

With mossy pillows beneath our feet,
Fungus and laughter mix up the treat.
A ladybug sings, in joyous tune,
Under the watch of a friendly raccoon.

In this joyous realm, let mirth take flight,
Where every leaf plays, from morning till night.
The forest floor breathes, alive in its glee,
Come join the fun, it's a wild jubilee!

Echoes of the Burgeoning Wild

In the thickets, giggles abound,
Bouncing squirrels make merry sounds.
The trees sway lively to a hidden beat,
While grasshoppers boogie on leafy seats.

A towering sunflower dons its crown,
While ants share tales of the day's renown.
I saw a hedgehog in shades, quite bold,
Swishing its tail, like royalty, gold!

With every rustle and playful leap,
The wild whispers secrets, promises to keep.
A butterfly joins in the merry spree,
Spreading joy with colors, just wait and see!

Let echoes roll through the flourishing wood,
Where laughter thrives, and all is good.
In this vibrant space of chirps and squeals,
Join the fun, embrace what nature reveals!

Journey Through Flourishing Greenery

Amidst the leaves, new friendships bloom,
As chipmunks race, dispelling gloom.
With acorns chattering, the gossip flies,
While fireflies waltz under starlit skies.

A cactus joins, with a comical smile,
While hedges gossip in a leafy style.
A turtle in sneakers, oh what a sight,
Casually gliding, feeling just right!

In the blooming patch, the daisies gather,
To share slapstick tales with uproarious laughter.
A gecko in shades does flips and spins,
All celebrating the joy within!

Through flourishing greenery, fun's the decree,
Where every creature sings, "Come dance with me!"
Embrace the chuckles, let your heart see,
In this vibrant wonder, we all can be free!

The Rebirth of Spring

Little bunnies hop around,
Chasing shadows on the ground.
Flowers bloom and then they sneeze,
Pollen dances on the breeze.

Chickens try to lay their eggs,
But they're just two silly pegs.
Sunshine laughs and gives a shout,
"Come outside! You can't pout!"

Trees put on their leafy hats,
Squirrels plan fun acrobats.
Nature throws a little ball,
And everyone has a ball.

Weather plays a playful trick,
Rainy days? Just a quick flick!
With every chuckle, warm delight,
Springtime is a pure delight.

Poems of the Petals

Petals swirl in breezy dance,
Bees are in a pollen trance.
Dandelions wear their crowns,
While tulips make silly frowns.

Lemonade stands in pure bliss,
Selling sips with lots of fizz.
Kids tripping over their own feet,
"Hey, watch out!" they laugh and greet.

Butterflies play tag in the sun,
Each one thinks it's just such fun.
Ladybugs in polka dots,
Posing nicely for their shots.

Even the rain drips with glee,
As it splashes the doggie, whee!
Nature sings in cheerful bursts,
Making merry, quenching thirsts.

Meadowstoft Place

In Meadowstoft, the grass is tall,
A rabbit gym, they leap and sprawl.
They throw a party, just for fun,
Where every guest can hop and run.

Cows wear sunglasses, looking cool,
While pigs swim in the muddy pool.
Chickens strut with sassy flair,
Declaring that they just don't care!

Horses play poker with some crows,
But crows cheat, as everybody knows.
Even trees start to sway and clap,
When wild winds take a fun little lap.

The sun sets in a boisterous hue,
As stars giggle, peeking through.
In Meadowstoft, there's always fun,
A silly world for everyone!

In the Thicket's Heart

In the thicket, secret spies,
Squirrels giggle, watching flies.
Raccoons in their bandit masks,
Complete their mischief, what a task!

Bushes hide a jumping game,
Frogs leap past without a name.
Owls chuckle, winking sly,
Underneath the moonlit sky.

A hedgehog prances, looking spry,
While flowers ask, "Oh me? Oh my!"
The thicket fills with silly glee,
As rabbits break into a spree.

Whispers of a secret song,
Where everything feels joyful, strong.
In the heart, laughter's embrace,
Is where fun finds its perfect place.

Vistas of Verdure

In fields of tall grass, I trip and fall,
Chasing a squirrel, I hear its call.
The daisies giggle, the sunflowers wink,
Nature's a prankster; I stop and think.

A rabbit hops by, with a cheeky grin,
Stealing my sandwich, oh what a sin!
But laughter erupts as I watch him flee,
Life in the leaves is a comedy spree.

The trees hold secrets, they whisper and sway,
I'm but a jester in nature's play.
With every step, there's a quirk to find,
In this realm of green, I leave cares behind.

So let's dance in the sunlight, take a chance,
Join the frogs croaking their silly romance.
In the land of the playful, beneath skies so blue,
Even the flowers know how to have fun too!

The Presence of Flora

Oh, the flowers are gossiping, can you hear?
They talk about bees, they laugh without fear.
Petunias and lilacs, all in a fuss,
In this blooming drama, it's always a plus.

A cactus rolls by, says it's feeling prickly,
Wants to join in, but oh, so sticky!
While orchids parade in their fancy attire,
It's a garden of laughter, none dare to tire.

The daisies declare it's a fashion contest,
With roots in the ground, they feel quite the best.
But amidst all the riffraff, a weed shows up,
Hilarious, yet it drinks from the same cup.

So here in this meadow of jests and delight,
The flora's alive, a whimsical sight.
Where blossoms are bloopers, and stems are a tease,
Life's just a garden, let's spread the unease!

Caress of the Wilderness

The vines like to tickle my ankles and feet,
As I wander the trails where wild things meet.
Fungi hold parties under large shady trees,
While critters converse on the hum of the breeze.

A raccoon in shades sipping water with flair,
Begs me to join in, irritates my hair.
The frogs in their puddles are croaking a tune,
They're the singers of spring, under light of the moon.

The bushes are bustling, what's happening here?
A squirrel plays tag, and launches a beer!
With laughter as fuel, the wild things unite,
In this raucous arena, there's never a fright.

So prance through the thickets, where mischief is grand,
In the caress of the green, it's a hilarious band.
With giggles and squirrels, take a moment to pause,
In this wilderness wonder, we'll give nature applause!

Taming the Wild

I tried to plant corn, but it came out in curls,
My garden's a jungle, with topsy-turvy swirls.
The carrots conspire and the potatoes revolt,
Vegetables chat, in a vegetable jolt.

A gopher hangs out, with a hat made of grass,
Claims he's the king, let's all raise a glass!
While peas roll in laughter, the tomatoes blush red,
What's tamed in the wild? A farm in my head.

The zucchini dance moves make me question my skills,
Their rhythm is dorky, it gives me the chills.
Pumpkins are giggling, plotting a heist,
To steal all my laughter, oh isn't it nice?

So come to the garden, let's all have a ball,
In this tame little world, we'll laugh through it all.
With soil on our shoes and a grin on our face,
Let's conquer the wild, in our own silly space!

Explorations in the Verdant Oasis

In a land where the bushes seem quite alive,
A squirrel in a suit starts to thrive.
He juggles acorns, oh what a sight,
While the birds applaud in sheer delight.

A turtle in shades takes a slow stroll,
Chasing after dreams, that's his goal.
With a wink and a nod, his shell so bright,
He teases the breeze, what a funny sight.

The flowers gossip about the tall trees,
While buzzing bees dance with the breeze.
A frog tells tales of the clouds above,
Of sticky situations and stories of love.

In this oasis, joy takes its flight,
With critters all laughing, feeling just right.
A party of nature under the sun's glow,
In the heart of the green, where the wild things go.

Emerald Dreams

A rabbit in boots hops with flair,
Chasing after dreams without a care.
His carrot cane points toward the sky,
As he dreams of being a pop star, oh my!

The daisies giggle when they see him dance,
They sway to the rhythm, giving him a chance.
With every twirl, he lets out a cheer,
As butterflies gather, lending an ear.

The mouse on a skateboard zooms past the trees,
Waving and laughing, he's a sight to please.
His tricks all amaze, his flips make him proud,
As the woods erupt in laughter so loud.

Underneath the stars, they all gather close,
Sharing sweet tales of their wildest hopes.
In emerald fields where the giggles resound,
Life's just a joke, in this joyful ground.

Verdant Whispers

The grass tells secrets in whispers so sly,
As the ants march proudly, reaching the sky.
They're planning a party, oh what a feast,
With crumbs and jokes, they're never the least.

A cat in a hammock starts to unwind,
Dreaming of tuna, he's lost in his mind.
But a playful breeze flips his nap on its head,
He's off like a rocket, no more sleepy dread!

The willows giggle in the cool summer shade,
While the frogs in the pond practice serenade.
Their croaks harmonize, a comical sound,
As the fish wiggle and dance all around.

In verdant corners where laughter won't stop,
Nature's a stage, it's the ultimate flop.
With each little creature playing their part,
In this playful haven where joy springs from heart.

Beneath the Canopy

Beneath leafy shields, the fun takes its stand,
Where monkeys play tag, swinging hand in hand.
They giggle and jump, a chaotic ballet,
As they plot their next prank, what a wild play!

The wind whispers jokes to the roots of the trees,
Tickling the bark while chatting with bees.
A hedgehog tries laughing, it's quite a rare feat,
With spines that wobble, he can't find his seat.

The mushrooms are lurking, all painted so bright,
They're holding a contest for the best silly sight.
An owl serves as judge, perched high on a limb,
As the best funny face makes his night grim.

So when wandering through and the laughter erupts,
Remember the fun that the forest erupts.
Beneath this green laughter, life's a great game,
With joy overflowing, and humor untame.

Pastures of Paradise

In fields where the cows wear shades,
They moo to the beat of the sun's parades.
The sheep hold a lottery with sprigs of clover,
While goats start a band when the day's almost over.

The pigs throw a dance on the mud-slicked floor,
With music from roosters who shout, "Encore!"
Grasshoppers wear tuxedos, slick and neat,
As frogs leap in rhythm with slippery feet.

Ducks quack in harmony, a comedy show,
Swapping jokes with the chickens, as only they know.
The breeze swirls around like a playful little ghost,
In these pastures of laughter, we all love the most.

So if you find trouble, just look to the fields,
Nature's the jester, and joy is revealed.
With a wink and a grin, nothing could be wrong,
In this comic green haven, we all sing along.

The Fabric of Leaves

The trees wear a patchwork of sunshine and shade,
While squirrels in bowties do acrobatics, well-played.
Leaves whisper secrets with tickles and laughs,
As branches sway dressed up in nature's fine gaffs.

A rabbit runs fashionably late for a feast,
His carrot-topped crown, a royal at least.
Fungi are dancing, their caps in a spin,
Inviting all critters to join in the din.

A parade of ants, in a single file line,
March past the daisies that claim they can shine.
The wind plays a tune, with a playful little tease,
In this verdant tapestry, everyone's at ease.

So let's raise a leaf, to the quirky and bright,
In this fabric of giggles, everything feels right.
With nature as our stage, come join in the fun,
Laughing with the leaves, 'til the day is done.

Oasis of Tranquility

In a patch of wildflowers, bees hold a ball,
Spinning with petals, they twirl and they sprawl.
The ladybugs gossip on stems with great bold,
Swapping stories of weather and treasures untold.

Turtles in shades lounge 'neath umbrellas of clover,
While crickets recite all their lines, it's a takeover!
Egrets try modeling their new feathered lines,
Claiming the spotlight, as the sun brightly shines.

Youthful sprigs of grass giggle as they grow,
Tickled by breezes with each gentle blow.
Here laughter mingles with each breezy note,
In this peaceful retreat, all worries float.

So come take a seat, in this serene little nook,
Where the critters share jokes like a well-written book.
In this oasis of joy, let your troubles take flight,
And savor the laughter that dances in light.

The Symphony of Greens

Among the lush greens, an orchestra's found,
Where the frogs croon tunes, and the cicadas surround.
With branches as violins and leaves as the score,
Nature's a concert, who could ask for more?

The flowers all sway like they're part of the dance,
While sunflowers lead moves, giving all a good chance.
A raccoon plays drums on a hollowed-out log,
With a magic routine involving a frog.

The sky adds its melody, gentle and bright,
As squirrels conduct from their perch with delight.
Even the shadows, they dance in the groove,
In this symphony of greens, we all start to move.

So grab your neighbors, it's a wild bash,
In this forest of fun, there's no reason to clash.
With laughter and music, the world feels so fine,
In this vibrant concert, we all intertwine.

Symphony of the Sprouts

In a garden full of giggles, they sprout,
Dancing wildly, with no doubt.
Tomato hats and lettuce shoes,
Whispering secrets, sharing news.

Beets are playing tiny drums,
While carrots hum in funny sums.
The peas giggle, roll in rows,
As the laughter in the garden grows.

Radishes twirl like little dancers,
Chasing flies like little prancers.
With each wiggle, the fun expands,
Twirling greens in merry bands.

A symphony of life's delight,
Underneath the sun so bright.
Oh how they sing and sway with glee,
In this garden, wild and free!

Roots of Serenity

Beneath the surface, giggles sound,
As roots gather, they spin around.
Whispering tales of grasshopper's fall,
Poking fun at the hefty ball.

Earthworms wiggle, tickling their toes,
Cracking jokes that nobody knows.
Composting laughter, they quietly hum,
Debating what makes the best jam!

Roots entwine like a funny crew,
Dreaming of days when they flew.
Sharing gossip with the stones,
Creating a club, using funny tones.

In this underground realm of cheer,
They laugh at the world, year after year.
For in their fortress, the roots do play,
Rooting for joy, come what may!

The Dance of Moss

Moss in a tutu, waltzing with style,
Twisting and twirling, just for a while.
With a top hat made of dew so bright,
They caper and frolic into the night.

The mushroom band plays a quirky tune,
As moss spins round, like a lively monsoon.
Fungus floats by, with a jolly grin,
Encouraging all to join in the spin!

Underneath branches, they slide and glide,
With each little shuffle, their damp hearts bide.
Frog friends leap, in this green ballet,
Joining the show in a slippery way.

Oh, how they giggle with every leap,
In nature's theater, laughter creeps.
Here in the shadows, life's a theme,
As moss takes flight in a whimsical dream!

Under the Verdant Sky

Beneath the broad leaves, giggles reign,
Grass blades sway in an amusing train.
While dandelions wear crowns of fluff,
Tickling the noses, 'Oh that's enough!'

The sun beams down, with a playful wink,
Cacti stand tall, thinking they might shrink.
While daffodils gossip without any care,
Spreading stories through fragrant air.

Bumblebees buzz in a comical way,
Trying to dance, but they just sway.
Around the blooms, laughter echoes loud,
As petals chuckle in a floral crowd.

Under this canvas, so vast and spry,
Nature unfolds, making spirits fly.
For in this paradise, joy will lie,
Bathed in the warmth of the verdant sky!

Sowing Seeds of Hope

In a garden so bright, the weeds dance with glee,
One sprout claimed the throne, just as proud as can be.
With a wink and a smile, it brags of its height,
While the others all grumble, 'Why can't we take flight?'

With a shovel and rattle, the gardener arrives,
They chat with each plant, giving them high fives.
'Just water and sunshine, and watch what we'll bloom,'
But one sneaky root says, 'I prefer the gloom!'

The daisies tell jokes, the sunflowers wear hats,
They compete for the prize in the prize-winning chats.
A tomato's got talent, a carrot can sing,
In this patch of pure joy, everyone's a king!

Jewel of the Landscape

A patch of bright colors, like jewels strewn wide,
Every flower's a gem, hard to choose a side.
The roses are prancing, the lilacs are bold,
Yet the dandelions laugh, 'We're rich, 'cause we're gold!'

One petunia cried out, 'I'm the star of this show!'
While the daisies all chilled, just going with flow.
'But we make the bees buzz; we keep things alive!'
Said the pocket-sized blooms, 'We're the ones who thrive!'

As butterflies swirl in an odd little dance,
The grasses all giggle, who knew they had chance?
A sunbeam remarked, 'This is pure flower flair!'
While the clouds above whispered, 'Do they need some air?'

Canopies of Calm

Beneath the big branches, all the critters convene,
A squirrel tells stories of the things he's seen.
The owls hoot with laughter, the chipmunks all cheer,
While the mice serve up tea, 'It's raucous, I fear!'

The leaves sway with fun, as they gossip and sway,
'Today's just a picnic; can we play all day?'
A bumblebee buzzes, 'Oh, let's play charades!'
And the mushrooms all laugh, 'We'll join in the parades!'

The wise old tree chuckles at the ruckus below,
'You'll be my comedians, I'll give you a show!'
In this canopy rich, there's a circus in bloom,
Where the joy of the forest can lift any gloom!

The Gentle Undergrowth

In the soft mossy layers, the critters all creep,
While the shadows are giggling, they're plotting to leap.
A hedgehog in tune with a snail's slow ballet,
Slips under the ferns, 'Cause it's time to play!

'Let's stage a grand caper, a jolly good race!'
Chirps the merry bluebird, with a smile on its face.
While the flowers look on, like a crowd full of fans,
'You'll never outrun me, I've got speed in my plans!'

With laughter and joy, the forest unfolds,
The gentle are brave, as this tale here now molds.
For the fun never ends, in the underwood's embrace,
Where all can be silly, no time to lose face!

www.ingramcontent.com/pod-product-compliance
Lightning Source LLC
Chambersburg PA
CBHW070330120526
44590CB00017B/2844